What Type of Character Are You Hanging Out With?

What Type of Character Are You Hanging Out With?

Betty Alark

To order additional copies of this book, contact:
Xlibris Corporation
1-888-795-4274
www.Xlibris.com
Orders@Xlibris.com
87506

Contents

To the Great—I Am!

Prologue

The purpose of this book is to stimulate the readers mind toward awareness, to encourage the reader to think and make informed decisions versus making decisions based on feelings, emotions, and lack of self-control!

The book provides the reader with several depictions of stories and scenario analysis that capture the essence of the possible dangers and risks of hanging out with a "character" that you know very little about and being taken advantage of as a result.

The depictions vary in style, yet behind each depiction lays the same message—why it is important to know something about the "character" of the person that you are about to hang out with before entering into a relationship or becoming intimately involved.

Awaken

Males and females encounter one another every day—unaware of what's lurking inside one another's "character."

Upon making someone's acquaintance, how frequently is their character your focal point? How easily is your attention diverted away from their character via a smiling face, flattery, a witty clever conversation that sounds convincing and poses as their character?

Amid the everyday obstacles of living, do you slow down long enough to question the character of the one desiring to enter your space? Do you ask yourself, why does this character desire to enter my space?

What if behind all that smiling, flattery, and witty conversation lies the big bad wolf, a con artist, or someone waiting to devour your soul?

People pick you out of curiosity all the time; should you assume that their picking is without forethought, that their motives and intentions are sincere, or should you question their integrity?

I know, it's a sad reality to walk around maintaining a conscious mind-set of skepticism regarding people; to be on guard and put up a defense 24/7. Sounds like a real snore amid everything else you have to deal with in life. I mean you just desire to live life, have fun, live your dreams without all the hassle; however, when you think about it, encountering people is a big part of life. Males and females seek a partner in life, and it all starts with the game of "attraction," thus the venture down an untraveled road.

If you're not walking around living life with a mind-set of awareness regarding passersby and those desiring to enter your space, then you're in for a rude awakening, for there are many wolves lurking around in the world, looking to prey on someone that doesn't have that mind-set, to take advantage of your unawareness.

You need to be aware in this world, not innocently ignorant. Life is lived in the world, and every character in the world isn't "good."

Only you know what's lurking around in your character; you don't know what's lurking inside the character of someone else.

Awaken!

A Sheep Among Wolves

You, an innocent sheep, venture out into the world seeking to find yourself, unaware that the world is full of wolves disguised in sheep's clothing waiting to rob, steal, and devour your most precious possessions—your innocence, self-worth, your soul.

Along the path of your journey you meet various types of sheep, some similar to yourself and some different in character and personality. At this juncture on your journey as you're trying to find yourself, you haven't yet learned to distinguish a sheep from a wolf in sheep's clothing; you simply realize that characters and personalities of all types exist!

In reality the sheep and wolves are learning and growing up together—sheep being sheep, and wolves being wolves. When you come in contact with each other, you compare likenesses, differences, similarities, values, etc. You make determinations regarding the nature of each other. From time to time you become more sociable, more acquainted and personable with some characters than you do with others. You're learning life and yourself; you're having a good time!

As you continue exploring and experiencing life, trying to find your way, what becomes at stake and up for grabs as you reveal who you are to others are your most precious possessions—your innocence, self-worth, your soul. You, a sheep, go about your life just being the innocent that you are. As you make contact with other sheep and wolves in sheep's clothing, they are witnessing your identity. The nature of your being sends out vibrations that attract onlookers—sheep and wolves alike. They are drawn to your innocence, your spirit! Out of curiosity, they pick the essence of who you are. Some will come toward you with good intentions and some with intentions and motives that are not sincere.

There are givers and takers in this world. On some level we all are. We give and we receive. However, there are wolves in sheep's clothing that will have no regard for your most precious possessions—your innocence, self-worth, your soul.

A wolf that is out to rob, steal and devour won't look upon your most precious possessions as beautiful treasures to be cherished, as things of value; a wolf will move toward you to devour them for personal gain.

At this point of your life journey you haven't encountered a wolf whose intent is to test the core of your being, to shatter the nature of who you are. Until now you've just been out there testing the waters of life with your friends, having fun, socializing, becoming acquainted! You've probably had a few innocent, romantic flings; however, you haven't come across anyone who has tested the very core of your being, with the intent of bringing your soul straight down to hell.

Unexpectedly, out of the blue, suddenly it happens—you meet a character like no other! A charming character! This character appears to be a sheep. I say "appears to be a sheep" because you've never met a wolf in sheep's clothing. You haven't experienced enough of life for your discerning abilities to be sharp enough to distinguish a sheep from a wolf, nor have you been taught to. You like this character's charm, wit, appeal; in fact these characteristics captivate you. This character captivates your emotions, your flesh, by its mere appearance and words. Everything about this character practically mesmerizes you. It seems all the right buttons are being pushed, innocently unaware that this character is a wolf in sheep's clothing.

Now a wolf in sheep's clothing is a wolf, not a sheep. Its nature is contrary to that of yours—a sheep. Once a wolf detects your naivety, your innocence, a wolf will move in to devour your most precious possessions. To do so, a wolf will maintain a disguise—a wolf in sheep's clothing. A wolf will utilize strategies, tactics, and deceptions in order to keep you blind, captivated, and mesmerized while moving in to trap its prey.

So you're mesmerized, captivated by this charming character, so much so that your lack of experience and emotional blindness prevent you from summing up the true nature of the wolf's character. The only thing being detected by you is its charm, wit, and appeal, which to you is its character. You're thinking, and most definitely feeling, that this is a good sheep; and you're more than willing to have this character step into your world, your space! In your innocence and lack of experience to discern a wolf in sheep's clothing from a sheep, you venture in; you open the door for this character to come into your world, unaware that this disguised sheep is really a wolf.

Now the wolf is smacking and licking its chops, since the door has now been opened, and it can come in and devour its victim's most precious possessions.

A wolf won't stop and say, "Don't give me your most precious possessions; give them to someone who will cherish, value, and appreciate them." No, a wolf will welcome your invitation to come into your space in order to prey and take advantage of your innocence. Once the wolf is in your space, it will commence with its program to bring your soul down to hell; meanwhile, you're hindered by being emotionally blinded, mesmerized, and captivated by the light of this creature—this wolf, who's prancing around in sheep's clothing.

Innocently blinded by the light of this being (the wolf), you freely give yourself; after all, you thought it was a sheep when you opened the door and let it in. Revealing more and more of who you are to this master of intrigue, disguise, lies, and deception, the wolf learns your strengths and weaknesses, using them against you in order to devour your soul and bring you down to hell. First, the wolf will attack your emotions, beguiling you with its charm, wit, and appeal. Second, the wolf will attack your flesh, which is your greatest weakness. Knowing that you are emotionally blinded and attached, the wolf will constantly stroke your flesh, your intimate parts, which will ensure that you will stay by its side. Third, the wolf will attack your psyche attempting to lower your self-esteem, your self-worth, causing you to think little of yourself and enabling the wolf to move in to devour.

Once a wolf can devour you, then it can start pulling you down to hell, or at least, attempt to. Some victims fall deeper than others, depending on their strengths and weaknesses. If it can bring you to a place where you lose all self-respect, where you are so low that you're kept depressed, empty, and weak—where you really begin to believe that you have no self-worth, no self-value—then the wolf has shattered the core of your being, your psyche, "self." Even under a shattered psyche the wolf holds you captive by continuing to stroke your flesh, your intimate parts—your greatest weakness.

Thinking and feeling that you do love this master of intrigue, disguise, lies and deception you keep succumbing to the weakness of your passions, your flesh. Since you gave your innocent self freely to this creature, in all likelihood you started out sincerely caring for this creature. Blinded by your emotions, you were pulled in by deception; you were simply being true to the nature of yourself, and so was the wolf.

After a period of time (the duration being longer for some than others) a light starts to shine—you begin to see this wolf in sheep's clothing for what it really is. Your emotional bondage is beginning to wear off. Your eyes are being opened. You discern that the nature of this character is unlike your own that its intentions, motives, and disguise have all been deliberate intents to strip you of your dignity, self-respect, and self-worth; but finally you're waking up. Light is starting to shine through your soul; you haven't been brought so low by this creature as to have lost all sense of who you are, the true nature of yourself—a sheep! You're saying to yourself, "This character has led me somewhere where I don't want to be; I've somehow lost myself. However, I'm now being found."

As a result of your awakening, you long to be set free from the captivity of the wolf, to be brought back from the door of hell. Regaining your self-respect and self-worth is paramount on your list, and you're doing it; however, amid your awakening you realize that there are still remnants of the wolf's captivation that delay your departure from it. Your flesh, your greatest weakness, is still held captive. Well, your nature is what it is—sheep! You've loved and you've loved deeply; you've given and you've given freely at no cost, the essence of who you are, and yes, it hurts deeply to depart from the essence of what you've genuinely given. It's like leaving yourself behind.

The captivity of your flesh is the last hurdle to be overcome. The wolf isn't going to fling open the door of hell to release you, that's why it stroked your flesh, your intimate parts so well and often so it could assure your captivity. It's now up to you to call on your inner strength, courage, your higher power to rescue you, to put your flesh on hold by using self-control.

You now realize that the identity of this character in sheep's clothing is false. Its makeup consists of lies, deception, a false light. The wolf has no real power of its own over you; only the power of your own weaknesses that you gave it over you. You can only be made powerless and held captive by your own weaknesses—not that innocence is a weakness; however it can be used against you when your discerning abilities haven't been sharpened by experience and wisdom. So determine what is making you weak; empower yourself against it, and set yourself free!

Well, you've had quite a journey. You were swayed along the way, blinded along the path, even lost your way. Then a light came and shone through your soul to put you back on the path and show you the way! You might have acquired a few bumps, bruises, and scrapes along the way; however, you should be able to start out on your journey anew as a much wiser, stronger, discerning sheep. Remember, you set out to find yourself; even though you may have been dragged to hell's door, your soul awakened you, reminding you of your true nature—a sheep! You started out as an innocent sheep; now you're a more mature, stronger, discerning sheep. The nature of who you are didn't change, and that was the test, hidden though it may have been.

The wolf tried to destroy your soul—the nature of who you are. Keep that in mind, since along the pathway of life you will encounter many more wolves in sheep's clothing. Wolves in sheep's clothing are not easily identifiable. They can appear as angels of light; they wear many disguises and are masters of intrigue and deception. You will need to keep your ability of discernment sharp and not be fooled, mesmerized, and captivated by every light that shines before you. There's an old saying that goes, "Everything that looks good isn't good for you." So be watchful along the way. Be cautious about opening the door of your heart, the door of who you are to just anyone. Don't reveal yourself before knowing to whom you are revealing yourself to. A person may seem to be beautiful on the outside; however, that very character could be out to devour your soul and attempt to bring you down to hell.

Enjoy the rest of your journey!
Stay alert!

The Game of Attraction

What's your perception? How do you look at attraction? Do you look at it as a force that has power? When attraction happens to you, how do you identify with it? Or do you? Have you ever tried to figure out what attraction is? Normally, attraction happens unexpectedly! It sneaks up on you by surprise! It's like being hypnotized by some force; and when the power of its force comes upon you, it pulls you like a magnet. And like a magnet, attracts you to itself! The pulling doesn't feel bad, like you're being forced against your will; it feels good! That's pretty mysterious, don't you think? My point is, do you ever look at attraction like that—as a mysterious entity that has force and power, and draws two people to itself? The force and power don't stop pulling until the magnetism wears off. The attraction comes, has its way with you, and at some point in time, makes its exit!

What's to be learned from the power and force of attraction? Is that its purpose, for us to learn from it? My rationale is that attraction happens to you, and when something happens to you, it happens for a reason. I know everybody doesn't pay attention to attraction from a scientific point of view, especially while it's happening to you; however, my mind does. When attraction happened to me, I put it under the microscope. I observed and analyzed it. I didn't allow what I was feeling to overwhelm my sense of ability to observe attraction in action! From the moment of attraction, I detected its presence; I felt its force and power. I observed this entity affecting my being; however, its magnetic, pulling power didn't stop with me. It was also acting upon another, the one it was attracting me to, and vice versa. Thus, its purpose was twofold.

Even though I was being drawn toward a significant other and vice versa, my eyes were on the invisible force of attraction! Where was this unseen force coming from? It appeared to be coming from inside the two of us—the significant other and I, compelling us toward one another, affecting our senses, emotions, and impulses. It became difficult for me during those moments of having my attention diverted to what I was now feeling emotionally, to keep attraction under the microscope; however, my scientific mind was more dominating than my emotions, and I snapped back to the scientific mode! It was realized within those moments of diversion that attraction can be captivating, causing one's emotions to be in control versus using one's sense of ability to maintain a sound mind of reason.

Attraction was teaching me a lot about itself and about me! Then, I started to see the big picture. I had a clear vision of what attraction is and its purpose. We (the significant other and I) were attraction's "students" and it was our teacher! We were in life's school, and attraction had come to teach us some lessons! Attraction pairs two students up with one another, and then it begins to teach!

The Game

The lesson starts out as a game. The participants are the two students. The mystery of the game is that the character of each student is unknown to one another. There's one known factor in the game—that an attraction exists between the two participants. The pieces needed to play the game are reason, common sense, thinking abilities, and self-control. The degree to how each student will use the pieces that are needed is an unknown factor. Some factors that might come into play are gullibility, naivety, innocence, values, morals, motives, intentions, and emotions. There are two strategic ways the game can be played:

1. *Blinded by emotions and using no self-control*
2. *Based on using reason and using self-control*

How each student chooses to play the game is unknown to the other at the commencement of the game; however, that knowledge will be revealed as the game progresses. The outcome of the game is dependent upon the strategy used.

The objective is to teach its students how to play the game and how to play it well. There is a price for playing the game of attraction, and each person's character is the culprit. You enter the game at your own risk—attraction doesn't discriminate. It could pair up beauty and the beast, or vice versa.

Since the game of attraction is entered into with blinders on, your best strategy of defense would be not to enter the game until you know something about the character that's playing against you.

What the Game of Attraction Taught Me

Attraction taught me that it is a teacher that it comes to serve its purpose!

It brings two students together, and then the game begins. It taught me that it takes constant forethought to stay focused while under its magnetic force and power, the reason being that attraction isn't just a mental game; one's feelings, emotions and impulses do come in to play.

Attraction taught me that it's a matter of learning to control my emotional and physical impulses while I play the mental aspect of the game. It taught me that emotions obscure its real purpose; and while playing the game, if I put more emphasis on letting my emotions and physical impulses be in control then the outcome of the game will impact me differently than it would have had I used reason and control of my emotions.

Emotions obstruct your vision, and don't allow you to see behind the scenes—to see the true face of the character that you are playing against. Attraction taught me that I could enter the game of attraction with a conscious awareness of its identity and purpose; so when attraction comes knocking at my door, I can approach it objectively with the knowledge that a lesson is coming my way and I need to keep a tight rein on my emotions. Attraction taught me that I need to attack my opponent with a sound mind of reason versus entering the game emotionally; thinking that at some point down the road, attraction will get me my physical impulses satisfied. If you enter the game of attraction with that mind-set, your opponent could devastatingly defeat you without caring whether you're a rookie at the game or not. The objective of the game is to teach, and your lessons can result in paying a high price.

As a result of learning to control my physical and emotional impulses, I've come to appreciate the game of attraction and its purpose! The game can be fun—adventurous, and very challenging! However, I enter the game of attraction with caution and awareness, with the intention of learning who my opponent is and what type of character I'm going to be up against. I don't know the lesson that's going to come through my opponent, the one I've been paired up with; so I want to go in at a slow pace and see how my opponent plays, step-by-step.

Henceforth, before you play the game of attraction, think about the strategy you will use. Will you get to know something about the character of the person that attraction has paired you up with before you enter the game, or will you let emotions and lack of self-control be the driving force that determines the moves you make? Remember that attraction doesn't discriminate, and it could pair you up with beauty or the beast. Beware of the game of attraction.

Only Fools Rush In

The physical exterior of a person is the first thing seen by the eye of the beholder. It only takes a few moments to determine if you like what you see! It takes a much longer period of time to learn the unseen aspects of a person—their character, moods, emotions, personality, intentions, motives, values, the soul and spirit of the person.

Only the individual knows what's lurking inside their own character; hence, when two people find themselves attracted to one another, moving toward one another should be approached with caution! As the old saying goes, "Only fools rush in."

Scenario:

Two people come in contact with one another, there's a physical attraction. They talk briefly and phone numbers are exchanged. Days later, connection is made via telephone. Conversation is held several times over the phone before an agreement is made to meet in person.

Let's analyze two possible approaches prior to the two people getting together, and their outcomes.

Approach #1 Objective Approach

The objective approach calls for a seeker with a plan! A person who sets out for the meeting knowing in advance what their objective is, why they are going to meet this person, where they are going to meet, what questions they will ask, and what they plan on discussing.

It calls for a seeker who consciously sets out to discover, learn, and gain understanding about the character of the individual that they are meeting with.

It calls for a person that uses self-control; someone who's able to put their emotions on hold while they are obtaining information, making determinations, and drawing conclusions in order to make informed decisions about the individual.

It calls for a person to reason, experiment and challenge; someone who won't just accept what's being said.

It calls for a person that will put the subject (the person they're meeting with) under the microscope in order to study, probe, and ask questions.

The overall objective of the seeker is to study the person that they are meeting with long enough to find out what's behind the mask of attraction; to learn the personality and character of the person, before rushing into a relationship; to learn if down the road the two of you could be a compatible match for one another; to determine if the two of you share similar values, convictions, and commonalities; and to learn if the person that your meeting with is caring, loving, patient, humane, responsible, accountable, etc.

One of the main objectives within the objective approach is for the seeker to realize the importance of voicing to the person that she, or he is meeting with, (during the initial meeting) their objective for agreeing on the meeting. The person you are meeting with needs to be informed that the purpose for meeting is to become acquainted, that you are not interested in entering into a relationship right away—you are simply trying to discover if a relationship is possible at some point in time. The person that you are meeting with needs to be made aware of the fact that you didn't agree to the meeting to open yourself up emotionally nor physically; therefore, sexual advances aren't acceptable. Overall, it's important for the seeker to let the person they are meeting with know what their intentions are and what they will and won't accept.

It takes time to get to know a person. It's a lifelong process; however, it's extremely important to know to some degree prior to opening yourself up emotionally and physically to another person, what inhabits their spirit, and what type of character they have so that when you are ready to share your innermost self with that significant other, you will at least have some certainty that the nature of who you are, will be received by them with appreciation; that you as a person will be valued and respected!

The objective approach takes time. It's not an approach you can rush into. The two of you while becoming acquainted, can enjoy one another's company, have fun, indulge in conversation, and participate in events that allow the two of you to witness different aspects of one another, etc.

The objective approach provides both parties with the opportunity to make informed decisions regarding one another and to determine whether there's the potential for a potential relationship! Now let's consider the second approach.

Approach # 2 Subjective Approach

The subjective approach calls for a person that doesn't have a planned objective prior to meeting the person that they're attracted to. The attitude of the person using the subjective approach is they will meet, and just let nature take its course. The subjective approach calls for a person that doesn't use self-control over their emotions.

Scenario:

Two people come in contact with one another, there's a physical attraction between them. They talk briefly and exchange phone numbers. They communicate with one another via telephone several times before agreeing to meet. After a few times of getting together, the two people move toward one another too fast; they succumb to the power and force of attraction and their emotional impulses. Utilizing self-control of their emotions long enough to obtain vital information regarding one another's character, in order to make informed decisions, is never applied. They enter into a sexual relationship without really knowing one another.

There are risks, and possibly danger, for two people who are attracted to one another to enter into a relationship without first allowing enough time to get to know one another's character. Since it is the force and power of the attraction, and emotional impulses that binds them; not compatibility, values, nor commonalities.

When two people enter into a relationship based on the subjective approach, there's always the risk of one of the two people becoming emotionally and physically bonded; thus, feeling that the one they are attached to owes them some type of commitment. If the two people continue to unite themselves sexually there's the potential risk of the attached person becoming, progressively, emotionally, mentally, and physically attached to the emotionally, unattached person. As the sexual attraction wears off, the two people come face-to-face with the reality that attraction was the only factor that was keeping them together; that they shared neither commonalities nor characteristics that made them compatible. Realizing that the relationship has no bases other than attraction, the emotionally unattached person could decide to leave the relationship leaving the emotionally attached person to deal with their emotions alone. Or, the *emotionally unattached person, could see the attached person's attachment as an opportunity to take advantage of the emotionally attached person- therein lies the real danger. By not getting to know the character of the person who now sees your attachment as an opportunity to take advantage of you, you have put yourself at risk to be a victim of that character's manipulation; to possibly be abused emotionally, mentally or physically.*

The subjective approach has numerous variations. Some cases can be more or less extreme; it simply depends on the nature of the person you are attracted to. The nature of a person (their character) determines the outcome of the events that occur within a relationship. Without knowing the nature of a person, what type of spirit inhabits that person, it can become a frightening reality to learn that the person that you are now attracted and attached to isn't a very humane person.

As mentioned, the subjective approach can have many variations; the outcome doesn't have to be as extreme as someone taking advantage of you in extreme ways. However, no one deserves being taken advantage of to any degree, especially when they sincerely give themselves to another person emotionally and physically.

So we learn that the objective and subjective approaches, when applied, have very different outcomes. The outcome is mainly based on the duration of time that is given to get to know a person's character before revealing who you are, and opening yourself up emotionally and physically. The objective approach isn't perfect since it takes a lifetime to really get to know someone. However, the objective approach can be a possible life-saving strategy, and act as a possible safeguard against any type of abuse and being taken advantage of. The objective approach provides you with time to make mental notes about the person you are becoming acquainted with in order to be able to make informed decisions, and determine if that person could be a potential and compatible match for you in the future and vice versa!

Going into any situation knowing that everyone's spirit, intentions and motives are not the same as yours, is going into a situation with your eyes open, not shut. The "self" can be so easily shattered by the inconsiderate, inhumane acts of other human beings. Using self-control of one's emotions far outweighs the detriment of emotional bondage, and having your flesh held captive by someone who doesn't care.

Next time you find yourself attracted to someone and you agree to get together, consider applying the objective approach as a seeker; in order to gain information regarding the character you are about to encounter, versus applying the subjective approach where you encounter one another being swayed by your emotions. Remember the old saying "Only fools rush in."

Love Is Something You Do,
Not Something You Feel

*I've heard it said that "love is something you do, not something you feel."
When I heard the saying, I was taken by surprise! I wasn't mentally acquainted
with love being something you do, I had always equated love with something
you felt emotionally! In order to gain a better understanding of the meaning
of the saying, I've decided to go on a research adventure in order to gain that
understanding, and to validate the saying.*

*Three sources of information will be used in order to gain an understanding
of the meaning of the saying "Love is something you do, not something you feel"
and to validate it.*

The first source will be *my past visual memories where I deemed myself
to be in love!*

The second source will be *to continue to analyze the saying "Love is
something you do, not something you feel."*

The third source will be the scripture*: 1ˢᵗ Corinthians 13:4-8*

*The pursuit begins with me revisiting the visual memories of my past,
where I deemed myself to be in love with a significant other! Looking back,
I witness myself and a significant other sharing aspects of ourselves with one
another; becoming intimately, emotionally, and physically involved. We shared
our innocence, gullibility, naivety, trust, sincerity, emotions, etc., though not
necessarily mutually. As I bear witness to the exchange occurring between the
two of us, I ask myself the following questions:*

*Am I witnessing love? Was the giving of ourselves in all the aforementioned
ways a validation of what love is, or did I deem it to be love based on
attraction, intimacy, growing fond of one another, and what I felt emotionally
and physically for the significant other? If that was the case, wasn't I simple*

engrossed with what I felt inside myself towards the significant other? Was that engrossment love?

As engrossed with one another as two people might be, is that an indication that there's a mutual exchange of what's being experienced, of what's occurring inside one another that will result in oneness, togetherness, commitment, friendship—something that's steadfast and lasting? Does it mean that the two people share the same hope of being together for the rest of their lives? If not, then how can what's being exchanged, given and received, between two people be validated as love? I then asked myself, what is love?

In view of the question let's analyze the words of the saying "Love is something you do, not something you feel," and determine whether or not the validity of those words held true in the case of myself and the significant other. Giving implies action! Action implies doing something. Interchange between two people requires giving and receiving, therefore action. Thus, it can be concluded that the significant other and I were "doing" something. What lies in question is the manner in which we gave ourselves to one another, and if what we felt was mutual. In order to determine if the words of the saying held true in our situation, additional information is needed—an understanding of what love is. Let's turn our attention to the scriptures, 1ˢᵗ Corinthians 13:4-8.

What is love?

First Corinthians 13:4-8 states that "love is patient, love is kind. Love doesn't envy, it doesn't boast, it's not proud. It's not rude, it's not self-seeking, it keeps no record of wrongs. Love doesn't delight in evil, but rejoices with the truth. It always protects, it always trusts, it always hopes, it always perseveres. Love never fails.

After reading and studying the verses, what conclusions can be drawn regarding love?

It can be concluded that

1. *love has a character of its own*
2. *love is a thing (love is referred to as an "it")*
3. *love is something that is put into practice*
4. *love is a set of principles or acts that are carried out*
5. *love is something you do, not something you feel*
6. *love is absolute*
7. *love is unconditional*
8. *if the principles of love are put into practice by a practitioner, the character of the practitioner represents the thing being put in to practice—love!*

9. *a person can know when they are acting in love and when they are not, via putting the principles into practice or not*

Now that an understanding of what love is has been gained, I'm equipped to determine whether the manner in which the significant other and I give ourselves to one another, held true to the meaning of the saying "Love is something you do, not something you feel." Before making that determination let's consider several pertinent factors:

In a relationship where two people are intimately and emotionally involved, and one or the other deems himself to be in love, there's always the hope of an outcome, something steadfast and lasting! When intimate, emotional attachment becomes a factor in a relationship, there's a need for the participants to know if they are experiencing something mutual. Decisions are made based on that factor, and mutuality is a variable in determining if the two people will share something that will be steadfast and lasting!

The description of what love is, stated in 1ˢᵗ Corinthians 13:5 states that love isn't self-seeking. What I interpret that to mean is that when an act of love is put into practice, it's done unconditionally; that nothing is expected in return for what's being given.

Reflecting back on my past visual memories when I deemed myself to be in love with a significant other, I can honestly say that I sought something in return as a result of giving myself in the manner that I gave. I had expectations of returned affection—time, commitment, being the only partner, and responsibility and accountability. My intimate, emotional attachment to the significant other validated and justified my expectations, at least in my mind. As a result of the continual joining of ourselves intimately, my mind and my emotions confirmed a confirmation of mutuality. However, that was an assumed conformation held inside my mind, until I woke up and became eyewitness to the contrary and asked for verbal confirmation of what I deemed to be true. I needed a verbal confirmation that confirmed that we had the same hope of the desired outcome of something steadfast and lasting together!

The outcome of what I deemed to be mutual ended in a severed relationship and I was left to feel what I felt inside myself, alone.

I'm fairly certain at some duration of our relationship we might have practiced at least several of the principles of love unto one another; for example, being kind to one another, and trusting one another. However, the outcome of putting into practice several of the acts of love, in addition to giving of ourselves to one another intimately and emotionally, didn't result in oneness, steadfastness or anything lasting.

After considering all the factors, I can now return to whether or not the manner in which the significant other and I gave ourselves to one another held true to the saying "Love is something you do, not something you feel." At any time in our relationship, if we practiced any of the acts of love set forth in 1st Corinthians 13: 4-8, then the acts held true to the saying "Love is something you do, not something you feel." However, what we felt toward one another was separate from what an act of love is. What we felt toward one another could have caused us to practice an act of love unto one another. However, a feeling in and of itself, isn't an act of love and doesn't hold true to the meaning of the saying. I base that on the following conclusions.

A feeling doesn't reap what it sows; it possesses no intrinsic guarantee that will produce an outcome of oneness, togetherness, friendship, commitment, or anything steadfast and long-lasting between two people. I further based that conclusion on the following two acts of love described in 1st Corinthians 13:4-8 verses (5 and 8).

1. *Love isn't self-seeking*
2. *Love never fails*

These two principles are in direct contradiction to what someone feels toward another. The contradiction being that a feeling can fail to bring about a desired outcome of something hoped for; something steadfast and lasting between two people. Furthermore, in all actuality when two people are intimately, emotionally involved with one another there is the hope of expectations.

Example*: commitment, no other partners, accountability, etc.*

The acts of love on the other hand, when put into practice, bear their own fruit; they reap what they sow; they don't fail to produce a desired outcome nor seek anything in return; love is an "act" that's put into practice; it's not a "feeling."

So how does putting the principles of love into practice produce an outcome that will reap the hope of an outcome of oneness, togetherness friendship, commitment, and something steadfast and lasting for two people; versus a feeling based on intimate and emotional attachment that doesn't guarantee the same outcome? In order to make that assessment, I put before you again the principles of love stated in 1st Corinthians 13:4-8.

(4)Love is patient, love is kind, love doesn't envy, love doesn't boast, love isn't proud,(5) love isn't rude, love isn't self seeking, love isn't easily angered, love keeps no record of wrongs,(6) love doesn't delight in evil, but with the truth,(7) love always protects, love always trust, love always hopes, love always perseveres,(8) love never fails

It's already been established that a person can know when they are acting in love and when they are not. For example, being rude versus not being rude to someone. Therefore, if a person isn't practicing the principles of love, then love isn't taking place.

First Corinthians 13:8 states that "Love never fails." I interpret that to mean that when a principle of love is put into practice, it will bear fruit; it's outcome will be successful, since love reaps what it sows.

Examples: If you sow patience, patience will be reaped; if you sow kindness, kindness will be reaped.

First Corinthians 13:5 states that "love isn't self-seeking." I interpret that to mean that when a practitioner of an act of love, puts the acts into practice that nothing should **be expected in return, since the acts of love will reap their own reward!**

Example: A mother and father teach and practice the principles of love with their young child. They patiently await the manifestation of what they taught and practiced with their child. The parents aren't expecting for the young child to manifest the practice of the principles of love before the child has developed and attained the ability to do so. They can't witness in the child what the child doesn't yet possess. They wait for their actions of love (via- teaching and practicing the principles of love) to reap their own reward!

It becomes obvious that in order for a person to put the principles of love into practice that the ability to do so has to be present. So how is the ability attained? As mentioned, a child can be taught the principles of love.

A person can learn to put the principles of love into practice via experience, experience is a teacher; and, a person can spiritually attain the principles of love! Either way, once the ability to put the principles of love into practice is attained, the principles become a part of the practitioner's character!

The principles of love can be carried out by one person. It's not a requirement for the principles to be carried out by two people for their outcome to reap what they sow. However, an act of love does require a receiver. A receiver of an act of love can be a friend, a stranger, parents, siblings, a child, spouse, etc. There's no limit as to how many acts of love a person can put into practice; that's *dependent upon the person's character, what that person has been taught, how that person has been developed, their experience and spirituality. The principles can also be put into practice by two people practicing them unto one another; regardless of the type of relationship.*

Example: friendship, marriage, courtship, etc.

The principles of love require being put into practice, un-begrudgingly. Example: Your neighbor is old and can't really get around like she used to. She needs a few items from the store and asks you if you would pick up a few things for her. You say yes; however, your facial expression and body language say it's nothing you really desire to do. The observer witnesses your unwillingness. Even though you go to the store, love isn't going to reap what it sows, since you didn't sow love; you sowed an unwilling, begrudging attitude. The outcome produces something other than love, thus the saying "Love reaps what it sows." So I reemphasize, in order to put the acts of love into practice, a person has to have attained the ability to do so.

Everyone hasn't attained that ability, nor been developed in that manner, which creates an imbalance and a lack of mutuality in relationships; thereby explaining why the outcome of oneness, togetherness, mutuality, commitment, bonding, and something steadfast and lasting isn't perfected in relationships.

Example: In a relationship, whether two people have bonded intimately or not, if one person has more of a character of love via putting the principles of love into practice than the other person, there's an imbalance in terms of one person's needs being met more so than the others. The degree to which a person possesses and displays a character of love varies, thus the imbalance of needs being met.

Balance is created when two people are meeting the needs of one another equally, or to such a degree, that the lack isn't creating a significant problem; what's being sown is sufficient.

Time is a factor in love reaping what it sows. It could take years, months, days, or moments for the reaping to manifest. However, since 1st Corinthians 13:8 states that "love never fails," the reaping will come! The time factor depends on each person's character and needs.

For example, two people in a relationship display a high degree of love via their character. They practice the acts of love unto one another often. They see one another's needs, and they meet them. Love reaping what it sows is reaped at a fast pace; since the result of having the need met is immediate, the reaping is immediate or soon after!

Neither practitioner of love is looking for anything in return for having their needs met, since each practitioner is where they are in their development and understands the workings of putting the principles of love into practice. They possess a character of love and they do what comes natural to them; versus a situation where only one person in the relationship possesses and displays a character of love, which creates an imbalance of needs being met. In this case, where only one person in the relationship possesses the character of love, the reaping of what's being sown by the practitioner, will take a longer duration of time to manifest itself since the receiver is being taught how to develop a character of love; thus learning how to meet the needs of another. In both cases the person(s) who possesses a character of love isn't expecting anything in return, since the person meeting the need of the receiver understands that you can't receive from someone what they don't possess. If the person doesn't possess a character of love, what you hope to see won't manifest itself until what's being sown is reaped in that person; thus the meaning behind the saying "Love isn't self-seeking" since it produces its own reward!

Now, in answer to the question: "How does putting the principles of love into practice bring about the desired result of oneness, togetherness, commitment, something steadfast and lasting?" The more balance there is in terms of two people being able to meet one another's needs in a relationship via committing the acts of love unto one another, the more compatible they are. They share the same commonalities, values, and a mutual understanding of how things work. They are a compatible match for one another - why look elsewhere?

When two people are constantly committing acts of love unto one another, appreciation is the end result! Appreciation of someone's acts draws you closer to that person. When there's that near equal balance of having one another's needs meet, the hope of something steadfast and lasting manifest! With the exception of love reaping what it sows, nothing is a hundred percent perfect or guaranteed; for example, seldom do you meet two people that are on the exact same level at the same time. However, two people can come close, and having room to grow with one another is also appreciated!

I deemed myself to be in love many times. I based being in love on what I felt inside myself for the significant other. After gaining the understanding of what love is, I can honestly say that it was my emotions and physical involvement with a significant other that caused me to think that I was in love since it has been proven that love is something you do, not something you feel. That's not to say that feelings don't play a major part in two people becoming fond of one another, and having something steadfast and lasting; I say that because I can have a character of love and commit acts of love unto everyone that I come in contact with, it doesn't mean that I have feelings for everyone that I come in contact with; or that any one of those people will become my lifelong partner.

There are other factors involved in two people having a steadfast, lasting relationship. There's being attracted to one another, and developing feelings for one another; that's important when the attraction and feelings are genuine. However, it's the principles of love that are committed unto one another in addition to the attraction and what two people "feel" toward one another, that's going to have the greatest benefit in assuring that steadfastness, since the act of love is going to reap what it sows. Feelings based on attraction, emotional and sexual involvement don't come with that guarantee.

Summary:

As a result of gaining an understanding of what love is and what it isn't, it can now be understood what love produces as a result of being put into practice!

1. It's learned that when a principle is put into action (sown) that something is reaped as a result!
2. What's being sown is meeting the need of someone!
3. The receiver of what's being sown benefits from having the need met, and witnesses the act of love happening to them!
4. When people's needs are met, people become thankful and appreciative, and grow fond of the practitioner!
5. The principles of love aren't based on feelings since the receiver of an act of love could be a perfect stranger.
6. Love isn't self-seeking, it doesn't look for anything in return; love has its own intrinsic reward!
7. Love is something you do, not something you feel.

Conclusion

Life is a process! We all develop at different stages and at our own pace. Our character development is based on what we are taught, how we are developed, our environment, experiences, and our spirituality, etc. It would certainly be beneficial if everyone at an early age were taught the principles of love set forth in 1st Corinthians 13:4-8, thus developing a character of love. However, we've learned that imbalance in relationships proves otherwise.

In pursuit of writing this chapter, I've gained a great understanding of what love is! I can now go forth with a greater knowledge of how to show love *to someone, and perhaps be matched with a significant other who's attained the ability to to put the principles of love into practice! My hope is that you will too!*

There's power and beauty in the principles of love described in 1ˢᵗ Corinthians 13:4-8. My hope is that you will read, study, and apply them so that you will reap what love sows in all your relationships, and develop a character of love! When you have developed a character of love, wait and match yourself with someone who has attained the same; thus, assuring more of a balance within the relationship! Don't rush in—love reaps its own reward and is worth waiting for! Love reaps what it sows!

A Bonding of Oneness versus Emotional Bondage

Sexual intercourse can occur between two people under numerous circumstances. Examples:

1. *Age*
2. *Impulsiveness*
3. *After courtship*
4. *Consensually*
5. *Lack of self-control*
6. *Attraction*
7. *Emotional bonding, etc.*

Several things take place during the act of sexual intercourse: two bodies join together physically becoming one body. Their intimate parts connect. After the joining of the physical bodies, sensation, excitement, and pleasure are experienced, and climax occurs.

Afterwards, the two participants lay relaxed, experiencing moments of ecstasy, meditating on what's felt individually, and for the significant other that participated in the act of sexual intercourse.

Experiencing sensation, excitement, pleasure, and climax are all a natural part of the process of having sexual intercourse. However, the joining of two physical bodies via sexual intercourse doesn't guarantee a bonding of oneness between two people. Two people can be fond of one another and enjoy one another during sexual intercourse without a bonding of oneness occurring.

Two people can be physically attracted to one another and experience extreme pleasure via sexual intercourse, yet not experience a bonding of oneness.

What happens in a case where one of the two participants joined in, sexual intercourse becomes emotionally bonded? For the person that bonds emotionally, the joining of their body with the significant other's body isn't looked upon as mere sexual intercourse; for that person, the joining is received and met as an intimate union where all that is felt for the significant other is consummated without reserve. The union is sacred; however, in the case where only one person bonds emotionally, the sacredness is only experienced by the one. The significant other experiences something contrary to the fact.

Under the circumstances where the sacredness isn't mutual, if the emotionally bonded participant continues to have sexual intercourse with the significant other, the end result could be progressive, emotional bondage; while the significant other continues to enjoy the pleasures of the act.

A bonding of oneness between two people takes place prior to sexual intercourse. Otherwise, sexual intercourse is just sexual intercourse where the natural process of experiencing pleasure, sensation, excitement, and climax occurs; and the risk of one or the other becoming emotionally and physically attached. If two people haven't bonded prior to sexual intercourse, then the two becoming one isn't in the mix.

Some of the components that "bond" two people and consummate oneness in a relationship are: committing the principles of love unto one another; developing a friendship; becoming fond of one another's personality and character; being attracted to one another, and sharing common values and commonalities.

When the two people are matched based on the components that "bond" them a sacred union occurs where all that is mutually shared is intimately meshed and blended together in oneness! Their bodies naturally invite one another to join intimately!

The intimate joining in sexual intercourse is the icing on the cake that consummates oneness! The two become one, and when their bodies separate, the oneness still remains!

Lying down and joining one's physical body with a significant other should never be taken for granted, especially when the end result for one of the participants could end up being emotional and physical attachment, leading to emotional bondage. The emotional detriment can be extreme.

In a relationship, before being joined to someone via sexual intercourse if your hope is that the outcome will be "oneness" then it's vital to know if what the two of you share is mutual. If bonding hasn't taken place prior to sexual intercourse, chances are the only thing the two of you share is sexual attraction.

Common sense seldom comes into play amid sexual attraction; however, when two people don't mutually share the components necessary to bond prior to having sexual intercourse, (even though there are rare exceptions) then they most likely won't, share them afterwards.

Oneness can be the most beautiful, sacred event that can be shared between two people; which is why its' important to know before joining yourself with someone via sexual intercourse, if the two of you have a mutual hope of attaining it. Otherwise, unless you're just out for sexual gratification, you could be leaving yourself wide open to experience emotional bondage.

I'd like to leave you with two analogies of two people becoming one!

Analogy #1

Two people becoming one is like: two streams of water merging and becoming one stream! Love meeting Love!

Analogy #2

To people becoming one is like: two sail boats set out to sail on different sides of the world; eventually they sail into the same ocean. Upon making contact, they sail into one another becoming one ship! Love meeting Love!

Do Unto Others As You Would Have Them Do Unto You

We all have weaknesses and fall short of being perfect. One imperfection of human beings is thinking more of oneself than others.

No human being desires to suffer at the hand of other people's injustices however, the world is full of people that commit acts of injustice against one another.

Example # 1

A person can have a sexually transmitted disease. Out of retaliation or a selfish need to be sexually satisfied that person passes the disease on to someone else; having neither respect nor consideration for the victim.

Example #2

A significant other cares deeply for you. You're fond of the significant other however, you don't share mutual feelings. The significant other comes on to you, desiring to have sexual intercourse with you. You realize how strong that person's feelings are for you, and that having sexual intercourse would complicate the friendship. However, rather than do the right thing and decline, you seize the opportunity to satisfy your own selfishness.

In the second example, the mentality of the person that didn't decline the significant others advance is "I simply gave that person what they wanted."

If you were the significant other couldn't you appreciate the person that you're coming on to saying "Look, I care for you as a person and a friend. I know how you feel about me however; I don't share those same feelings. I don't want to see you get hurt; having sex would only complicate matters for you. I'm not going to let you do that to yourself."

That's a true friend, or at least a person that respects you as a person, not someone out to satisfy themselves and who has no regard for you as a person.

Some of the consequences of people caring more about themselves than others are: innocent people becoming victims, emotional and physical trauma, death, people learning not to trust or care about one another, and seeing people for who they can be.

People justify their acts of injustice in numerous ways.

Examples:

1.   *I just did to someone else what someone did to me.*
2.   *I got them before they got me.*
3.   *It's a dog-eat-dog world.*
4.   *I'm thinking about myself, later for you.*

Human beings that display that type of character don't possess a character of neither love nor compassion for other human beings that enables them to put into practice "do unto others as you would have them do unto you." Their character is "it's all about me, me, and me."

It only takes one act of injustice committed against another person for retaliation to rear its ugly head and before you know it, retaliation spreads like wild fire. Thus, people reaping what they sow. One wrongdoing creates another wrongdoing, resulting in a vicious cycle of demise for all.

Parents raise sons and daughters. If a child isn't taught to "do unto others as you would have them do unto you" and to practice the principles of love set forth in 1st Corinthians 13:4-8, then that child's character will be contrary to "do unto others as you would have them do unto you," especially if there's no demonstration of parents doing the same.

Change starts with each individual! You can't change other people; people have to want to change. However, if what you're passing on to others is "do unto others as you would have them do unto you," then that's what will return to you. Acts of justice reap acts of justice!

Heartfelt conviction against committing a crime or wrongdoings against another person has to come from within a person. The law can convict a person of a crime or wrong doing against another person however, if there's no personal conviction of that person's heart and conscience, then there's no guilt, remorse, shame, nor inner conviction. A person can regret going to jail, however there's no guarantee that jail has an effect on the person's heart, nor conscience; the jail sentence is simply that, a sentence for wrongdoing.

The world is littered with people that experience no conviction inside themselves for crimes and wrongdoings committed against other people. A person that feels no remorse or conviction within themselves has no moral conscience. In all likelihood, a person with no moral conscience grew up receiving no consequence for committing wrong doings against others, and had no moral teachings.

"Doing unto others as you would have them do unto you" can be conceived of in a totally different light than from the perspective of doing what's morally correct unto another human being. It's taken out of context all the time. There are people that perceive the morality of the saying from their own self-centered perspective.

Example:

A person that likes to have pain inflicted upon him or herself goes out and inflicts pain upon someone else, and receives some type of sick satisfaction from the other person's suffering. Their justification is "I was just doing unto someone else what I would have them do unto me." Well, obviously that person is imposing their own personal preference against someone else that doesn't share the same preference; thereby committing an injustice against an innocent person, and making them a victim of their satisfaction.

"Doing unto others as you would have them do unto you" can be deemed as a moral and spiritual principle that when put into practice reaps its own reward. There are, however, all types of characters in the world that will take something beautiful and use it for evil purposes.

My hope is that you will see the principle of "doing unto others as you would have them do unto you" from a moral and spiritual perspective, put it into practice and start a chain of reaping justice for all!

Forgiveness

Forgiveness is an act of love. It's not always easy to forgive someone when they've treated you inhumanely, humiliated you, or hurt you in some way.

It takes being convicted of your own wrongdoings against someone else before you can forgive another person's wrongdoings against you, for therein lays the understanding of what it means to forgive!

Example:

When I was in high school I had a very close friend. We shared many secrets regarding our lives with one another. As we grew closer my friend began to share personal information with me regarding her family. She asked me never to expose the information to anyone else. Later in the year, I was having a conversation with a few classmates and I inadvertently let some of the information regarding my friend's family slip out. I didn't mean to reveal the information; I just wasn't thinking. As soon as I caught myself, realizing what I had done, I was frantic! I begged the girls not to repeat what I had said. Unfortunately, they did repeat it. The next day when I went to class, word about my friend's family had already starting traveling like wildfire. It had become a major gossip piece all over the school. I felt so bad regarding what I had done; and that was only the beginning of what I was about to come face-to-face with.

After class was over, I was walking down the hall when I saw my friend coming toward me. She was crying, I'll never forget the look on her face. She appeared so distraught and angry! It was in those moments that I realized the extent of what opening my mouth and revealing what my friend had told me regarding her family had created. As I witnessed her face, it revealed to me how my actions had affected another human being. She couldn't believe that I had exposed her family to public ridicule. In her eyes, I had violated her trust in me, and I lost a friend. Not only did I lose a friend, her family's personal life was exposed to the entire community, resulting in gossip and ridicule; not to mention her parents being upset with their daughter for exposing their business to me.

That was my first practical lesson in learning why it's important not to repeat something that someone trusted you not to reveal; even though it wasn't intentional.

It mattered to me that my careless action had caused me to lose my best friend, and how it had devastated her family. My heart slowly convicted me of what I had done wrong. As a result of being convicted, I felt the need to make amends. So I went to my friend days later and confronted her. I explained to her that my actions weren't intentional, that after some time had passed, the information just slipped out. I asked her if she would forgive me. Her response was, "I'm so angry with you right now, forgiveness isn't something that's even on my mind; I can never trust you again, things will never be the same." I asked her if she would allow me to apologize to her family. She started crying and said, "You've done enough already, leave my family alone." I sadly walked away with my head down.

It took a long time before things quieted down around school and the community regarding my friend's family. It wasn't until the following year that I was unexpectedly approached by my former friend. She came over to the lunch table where I was sitting alone and asked if she could join me. She expressed to me that it was difficult for her to even gravitate toward me. She also stated that she accepted my apology, and that she forgave me. However, she didn't think things would ever be the same between us since she felt she could never trust me again. She then got up and walked away. From time to time we would see one another in passing and wave or say hi. However, our friendship was never resumed. The one thing that I could be thankful for was that she accepted my apology and that she forgave me!

I had to learn to accept that losing my friend was my own doing. I had learned a major lesson that year, one that I never forgot. That lesson was just one of many that helped to shape my character from a practical, moral perspective.

What I've shared regarding my friend and I is an example of my need for forgiveness, as a result of hurting someone else. The next example is an account of me forgiving someone for hurting me.

Example:

Prior to becoming married to my first husband, my character had already been shaped and developed by the practical, moral, spiritual teachings learned during my childhood. My life experiences were my testing grounds where the *spiritual, moral teachings were taught and learned on a practical level; the arena where the literal teachings could be put into practice.*

When I met my first husband, my character was that of a passive, introverted, untarnished person whose idea of marriage was being swept off my feet by Prince Charming on a white horse, and living happily ever after. Little did I know at the time of meeting my husband that he would be responsible for blowing the Prince-Charming-on-a-white-horse fantasy to smithereens. Like someone throwing stones at a glass house, that fantasy would come tumbling down.

Prior to encountering my first husband, my morality had never been tested under circumstances of being treated inhumanely by another human being. The possibility of coming face-to-face with such a situation didn't exist within my character of innocence, so when I did come face-to-face with a situation that tested my humanity (via my husband) I met it with fear, like a child meeting a monster in the dark! I was petrified and in doubt that such a human being existed on the planet Earth.

My husband was a Vietnam veteran. He returned from the war as a very paranoid person, who had lost all faith and trust in everyone and everything. He harbored war memories that tormented his soul; he was tormented mentally and emotionally. He suffered from anxiety, resentfulness, vengefulness, hate, anger, frustration, and a confused sense of what he had become. He was out of touch with who he used to be, as a person; his sense of morality and humanity had been displaced. As a result, he needed some type of solace to feel whole and well again. Aside from his internal self, he had no place to dispose of all that tormented and traumatized his soul—to release what victimized him internally.

My husband observed me at the college campus that we attended for an entire year without my awareness of the fact before he approached me. Like a detective, he surmised my character and deemed it to be the perfect type on which he could channel his ravaged emotions. As a result of having the perfect type of character, I was to become his scapegoat on which he could pour out his scorn against the world. Experiencing my husband's scorn was nothing short of being in the outer limits of anything I'd ever experienced. The outer limits of his scorn was hell from where I stood.

War had turned my husband into a literal monster that drank and took drugs in order to numb his war-ravaged memories and pain. However, from where I stood nothing had been numbed by those devices, for it was during those times when he drank alcohol and took illicit drugs that all that tormented his ravaged soul was expelled against me. It was during those times that I felt like I was living in a war zone exposed to a real live enemy that was hell-bent on destroying who I was as a person. It was as if he were on a mission to destroy the fiber of my being. He wanted to break me down and destroy all that I represented. I was a passive person; society hadn't destroyed my innocence. I was still fairly naïve in my thinking regarding the world and I was an idealist!

Before my husband was drafted at the age of 18, he too had some of those same characteristics that I had, that defined his character. Being in the war destroyed those attributes in him—he no longer looked at the world with eyes of innocence, he was no longer naïve. When he witnessed a representation of those attributes displayed by me, he hated that image since it represented what he had lost and couldn't regain; so he tried to destroy what he conceived of as a false reality living inside me.

War had changed my husband's character. He went into the service with morals, values, and a sense of humanity. However, as a result of killing other human beings not unlike himself, who had families—his sense of humanity and morality were devalued. I can only imagine how empty and distraught he must have felt. He was sent back home after the war to live with who he now was as a person, and to function in the society as a normal human being. He had no sense of how to function in the world as a "normal human being." He himself had been taken to the outer limits of anything he had ever experienced, and then dropped back into "normal society" as a walking time bomb who had no idea how to defuse the bomb. I became the victim of that time bomb every time it exploded. I was treated like the enemy, as if I wasn't human to him—had no value, no self-worth, and that's how he made me feel. Being exposed to such aggression belittled me as a person, lowered my self-esteem, and I started feeling like I had no self-worth. Eventually, I became paranoid, resentful, frustrated, and angry. I was petrified of this human being; he was a literal monster that terrorized and filled me with fear.

I was almost brought to a point of hating this human being who held me captive in my own home. It was when I started feeling the emotion of hate that I realized that my own morality and humanity was being questioned; since hate is an emotion that can take you to depths where you might attempt to do things you never imagined you were capable of doing.

Until I found myself in the situation of being a scapegoat of someone's scorn and held captive in my own home, I'd never experienced the emotion of hate or any emotion that came close to it. Something inside of me fought not to be brought to such a level of hating a human being. I realized that I needed a defense against feeling that way, before I did something I would regret for the *rest of my life. I finally found the courage to call the police; they became my defense against my husband's inhumane treatment against me.*

Time in jail served as a consequence that postponed his treatment toward me; since he hated being closed in and detained, and didn't desire to be sent back. I utilized the service of the police as my defense several times, before we finally separated. Jail, however, didn't remove the memories of the killing stored in his mind; nor did it heal his tormented soul.

Even though I had been devastated by the treatment received by my husband, I became a stronger person; though not before suffering a nervous breakdown, paranoia, humiliation, ridicule, mental and emotional abuse, and defamation of my character. It took me quite a few years to recover from the trauma of being terrorized and victimized by my husband. I felt a deep, deep sense of resentment toward him for a long duration of time. That was over twenty years ago; today I've healed, and forgiven my husband's abuse against me.

Let me share with you why it is that I harbor no ill will against my former husband, and how and why I forgave him!

I loved the person that my husband tried to be, amid his internal turmoil! When he wasn't drinking and taking drugs, which wasn't very often, he showed signs of being able to be kind, gentle, and desiring to have a normal life. We actually had a lot in common! I was a nature person, and so was he. He loved whitewater rafting and camping outdoors! By nature we were a lot alike; had I met him before he went off to war, I believe we would have been a wonderful match for one another. Due to his ravaged soul, our marriage never had a chance. It never had the opportunity to blossom as a result of the internal hell he suffered inside his soul.

Although I never excused my husband's treatment toward me, I did, however, come to have a semblance of understanding regarding his internal hell. After all, he had put me through hell in order for me to experience what hell was like. I could certainly empathize with what it feels like to be treated inhumanely, and to suffer emotional and mental trauma as a result. I knew what it felt like to be treated as if I had no value, no self-worth to another human being; and to be brought so low by such inhumane treatment that it resulted in testing my own morality, integrity, and humanity. I knew what it felt like to have a shift in my consciousness where I was brought to a place of not being able to fathom an experience that took me to the outer limits of what I considered the norm.

In a way, he had caused me to experience a semblance of the emotions and trauma that he had experienced as a result of being treated so inhumanely. I think he wanted me to understand what he was feeling inside and his treatment against me was his way of getting that point across.

I'm sure being in a war and killing other human beings has to be the ultimate test of one's humanity, integrity, morals, spirituality, and values; causing a person to feel less than human. I can't begin to imagine how that must have made him feel, and I don't claim to have had an understanding of that torment.

His inhumanity troubled me more than anything that he had put me through. It hurt me deeply that a human being could treat another human being in such an inhumane manner. I felt wounded, and saddened for his soul. My own humanity empathized and sympathized with his internal need for redemption; his need to be rescued from his internal bondage. He had no idea how to erase or free himself mentally nor emotionally from the memories and reality of killing other human beings, and the effect that doing so had on his soul.

It was in understanding his ethical dilemma, my humanity and spirituality, and being able to empathize and sympathize with his ethical dilemma that allowed me to forgive his inhumane acts against me. I had to look beyond my own suffering to see his needs. That's not to say that it was ok for him to choose and use me as a scapegoat for his scorn against the world; no one deserves to be treated inhumanely due to someone else's unfortunate life experiences, I simply understood.

There are options for people who suffer from mental and emotional abuse; like for example, counseling. My husband didn't feel that counselors could relate to where he had been, thus not being able to help him. However, I believe it would have been an ulterior option that would have deterred his attention away from me being his scapegoat.

Ultimately, as mentioned, I understood enough in order to relate to his ethical dilemma. My soul was in touch with his sorrows, sufferings, and pain. I have to believe that, that's what makes us human-when our soul and spirit are in touch with someone else's; that it matters to us how that person is suffering, and to find the courage to forgive their inhumanity against us!

Later in my husband's life after we had separated and divorced, he called me and asked me to forgive him. I expressed to him that I had. Several years later he died. I'd like to think that he is now at peace!

I'm a much stronger person as a result of what I had to endure from my husband; most importantly, I've learned to protect myself against ever being a scapegoat as a result of someone else's misfortunes in life.

Forgiving someone doesn't mean that that person's character will change as a result; however, it could affect a person in a positive way. Forgiving someone is an act of love that represents the character of the forgiver!

My life experiences have taught me about forgiving, and how to forgive. Being convicted of my own wrongdoings unto others has helped to shape my character. It matters to me how I affect other human beings, and the effects of doing so. I'm saddened when that same humanity isn't present in others. Not that I look for humanity in return for any acts of humanity that I commit, my spirit is simply saddened when humanity isn't present in the actions of others.

My spiritual, practical morals have assisted in shaping and developing my character, and provided me with my sense of humanity. Amid the two, I am thankful for the lessons of being forgiven and learning how to forgive!

Epilogue

Throughout this book I've attempted to convey the same point of view from different perspectives with the hope of constant reinforcement being its goal!

It sometimes takes a constant knock at the door before someone awakens!

I have no control over how people conduct their personal lives; however, I care very much how human beings are treated mentally, physically, emotionally, spiritually, and humanely!

It is vital to be aware of the types of characters that roam the world that we live in and to protect ourselves against the violation of one's person that comes about as a result of a character's lack of compassion, humanity, morality, spirituality, etc.

I hope this book has provided you with something to think about, that it has in some way impacted your thinking to the degree that you will be more consciously aware of every character that finds a reason to enter your space!

www.ingramcontent.com/pod-product-compliance
Lightning Source LLC
Chambersburg PA
CBHW050349290526
45785CB00006B/2702